Christmas 1997

Dear Sue,

To remind you of the
"Garage", "Quebec" & America '97
"New York! New York!"

Lots of Love

Ann
xxx

P.S.
"Just cook - will yer!"

Pancakes & Waffles

by Cara Hobday
Illustrated by Jan Hill

First published in Great Britain in 1995 by
Parragon Book Service Ltd
Unit 13–17
Avonbridge Trading Estate
Atlantic Road
Avonmouth
Bristol BS11 9QD

ISBN 0-7525-0772-9

Conceived, designed and produced by Haldane Mason, London

Printed in Italy

Note: Cup measurements in this book are for American cups.
Tablespoons are assumed to be 15ml. Unless otherwise stated, milk is
assumed to be full-fat, eggs are standard size 2 (AA) and pepper is freshly
ground black pepper.

CONTENTS

TRADITIONAL SHROVE TUESDAY PANCAKES

MAKES 8

125 g/4 oz/1 cup plain (all-purpose) flour

1 egg, beaten

1 egg yolk

300 ml/½ pint/1¼ cups milk

3 tbsp melted butter

TO SERVE

2 tbsp caster (superfine) sugar

50 ml/2 fl oz/¼ cup lemon juice

200 g/7 oz strawberries (optional)

Shrove Tuesday is known as Mardi Gras (Fat Tuesday) in many parts of the world. This is the last day before the lean Lent period, when you can go to town on your dessert – a good excuse to put some cream on top, I'd say.

1 Sift the flour into a bowl. Make a well in the centre and add the egg, egg yolk, milk and 2 tablespoons of the melted butter. Draw in the flour. Whisk together well and leave to rest for 30 minutes.

2 Brush a medium frying pan (skillet) or pancake pan with a little of the remaining butter and place over a medium heat.

3 Hold the hot pan in one hand and the pancake batter in a measuring jug in the other.

Tilt the pan and pour in about 50 ml/2 fl oz/ ¼ cup of the batter, tilting the pan immediately in the opposite direction so that the batter coats the base before it sets – you have to be quick.

4 When the batter has dried out on top, about 1 minute, turn the pancake over to cook on the other side – or, to impress your hungry family, toss it. To do this, hold the pan with one or both hands, tilt it away from you, shuffle the pancake towards

the far edge and flick it up into the air, and do your best to catch it. It doesn't have to go up very high, but do not hesitate otherwise the walls and floor will be spattered! Repeat with the remaining batter.

5 Turn on to a warm serving plate, sprinkle with sugar and squeeze over the lemon juice. Roll up and serve – with fruit, if preferred.

5

RATATOUILLE PANCAKES

These are a speciality of the Breton region of France, where they are always served in a square shape. The buckwheat adds a sour flavour to the pancake, and is an ideal complement to these fillings.

SERVES 4

4 tbsp olive oil
1 red onion, sliced
3 garlic cloves, crushed
1 aubergine (eggplant), diced
2 courgettes (zucchini), diced
1 orange (bell) pepper, diced
2 tbsp tomato purée (paste)
400 g/13 oz chopped tomatoes
1 tbsp chopped fresh dill
1 tbsp chopped fresh parsley
salt and pepper

BATTER

60 g/2 oz/½ cup plain (all-purpose) flour
60 g/2 oz/½ cup buckwheat flour
2 eggs, beaten
300 ml/½ pint/1¼ cups cider
60 g/2 oz/¼ cup butter, melted
oil for brushing

1 Heat the olive oil in a large pan, add the onion and garlic, and cook until soft, about 5 minutes.

2 Add the remaining ratatouille ingredients. Bring to the boil and simmer, uncovered, for 40 minutes, stirring occasionally.

3 Meanwhile, make the batter. Sift the flour and buckwheat flour into a bowl with a pinch of salt. Make a well in the centre and add the eggs, cider and melted butter. Draw in the flours and whisk together well. Set aside for 10 minutes.

4 Taste the ratatouille for seasoning. Cover the pan and turn off the heat.

5 Brush a frying pan (skillet) or pancake pan with a little oil and place over a medium high heat. Tilt the hot pan and pour in about 120 ml/4 fl oz/½ cup of the batter, tilting the pan immediately in the opposite direction, so that the batter coats the base of the pan before it sets.

6 When the batter has dried out on top, about 3 minutes,

flip the pancake over to cook on the other side, about 1 minute. Repeat with the remaining batter to make 4 fairly thick pancakes.

7 Spoon some ratatouille mixture into the centre of each pancake and fold in the 4 sides like an envelope so that a square shape is formed. Slide on to a warmed serving plate and serve piping hot.

BRETON BUCKWHEAT PANCAKES

If you ever pay a visit to Brittany, don't leave without sampling the deliciously sweet local mussels. In this recipe, they are served in buckwheat pancakes.

SERVES 4–6

1 kg/2 lb mussels in their shells

4 whole garlic cloves

30 g/1 oz/2 tbsp butter

2 shallots, chopped finely

400 g/13 oz chopped tomatoes

1 tsp saffron threads, crushed

3 tbsp white wine

1 tbsp single (light) cream

2 tbsp chopped fresh parsley

BATTER

60 g/2 oz/½ cup plain (all-purpose) flour

60 g/2 oz/½ cup buckwheat flour

2 eggs, beaten

300 ml/½ pint/1¼ cups dry sparkling cider

60 g/2 oz/¼ cup butter, melted

salt

oil for brushing

1 Clean the mussels, removing the beards. Discard any mussels that are open.

2 To make the batter, sift the flours into a bowl, make a well in the centre and add the eggs, a pinch of salt, the cider and melted butter. Whisk together well and set aside for 10 minutes.

3 To make the sauce, put the mussels into a large saucepan with 150 ml/¼ pint/⅔ cup water and 3 of the garlic cloves. Cover and simmer for 7–8 minutes. Remove from the heat and drain, reserving the cooking liquor. Set the mussels aside, discarding any that are still closed. Shell the mussels, reserving 8–12 in their shells for garnish.

4 Return the cooking liquor to the saucepan with the butter, shallots and the remaining garlic clove, crushed, and cook until the shallots have softened, about 3 minutes. Stir in the tomatoes, saffron, white wine and cream. Cook for 8–10 minutes until the liquor is reduced. Stir the mussels into the sauce. Keep warm over a low heat.

5 Brush a frying pan (skillet) or pancake pan with a little

oil and place over a medium high heat. Tilt the hot pan and pour in about 120 ml/4fl oz/½ cup of the batter, tilting the pan immediately in the opposite direction, so that the batter coats the base before it sets.

6 When the batter has dried out on top, about 3 minutes, turn the pancake over to cook on the other side, 2 minutes. Slide on to a warmed serving plate. Repeat with the remaining batter. Makes 4–6.

7 Spoon some sauce into the centre of each pancake. Fold up the 4 edges like a loose envelope. Garnish with the reserved mussels, sprinkle with chopped parsley and serve.

POTATO PANCAKES WITH SAUSAGES

This is a hearty, tasty dish for a winter's day. Toulouse sausages are strongly flavoured with garlic and are widely available, but if you are unable to find any, use ordinary sausages.

SERVES 4

60 g/2 oz/½ cup plain (all-purpose) flour

1 egg, beaten

1 tsp oil

300 ml/½ pint/1¼ cups milk

300 g/10 oz/2 cups white potatoes, grated

olive oil for brushing

FILLING

1 tbsp olive oil

500 g/1 lb Toulouse sausage, cut into 2.5 cm/1 inch pieces

1 celery stick, sliced

350 g/12 oz/4 cups Savoy cabbage, shredded

salt and pepper

1 Sift the flour and a pinch of salt into a bowl. Make a well in the centre and add the egg, oil and milk. Whisk together well. Set aside for 30 minutes, then stir the grated potato into the batter. Use immediately.

2 Brush a frying pan (skillet) or pancake pan with a little olive oil and place over a medium high heat. Make 2 small pancakes at a time, using about 50 ml/2 fl oz/¼ cup batter for each one, or 1 large pancake, using 120 ml/4 fl oz/½ cup batter. Cook both large and small pancakes for 3–4 minutes on each side, and stack on a baking sheet to keep warm, covered.

3 Heat the 1 tablespoon olive oil in a frying pan (skillet), add the Toulouse sausage and cook quickly, stirring constantly, until sealed on all sides. Add the celery and the cabbage, reduce the heat to medium and cook for 5 minutes. Season well.

4 Put 3 small potato pancakes or 1 large pancake per person on to each warmed

serving plate and spoon over the
Toulouse sausage mixture. Serve
piping hot.

GRAVADLAX PANCAKES

Gravadlax is marinated salmon, and it is used here to make a sophisticated supper or brunch dish. The dill flavour in the marinade should be quite strong.

1 Combine the sugar, dill, oil, lemon juice and mustard in a non-porous, non-metallic dish. Slice the smoked salmon and lay it in this marinade. Sprinkle over the salt and pepper. Leave to marinate for 1½ hours in the refrigerator. Remove and let it come to room temperature.

2 To make the batter, sift the flour into a bowl to aerate it and make a well in the centre. Add the remaining ingredients and whisk together well. Leave to rest for 30 minutes.

3 Brush a frying pan (skillet) or pancake pan with oil and place over a medium high heat. Spoon 3 tbsp of batter into the hot pan, to make one 10 cm/4 inch pancake. When the top of the pancake has dried out, about 2–3 minutes, turn it over to cook on the other side for a minute or so. Make 8 pancakes. Stack the pancakes on a baking sheet, cover and keep warm.

4 Put 2 pancakes on to a warmed serving plate. Spoon on a quarter of the cucumber and a quarter of the salmon. Repeat with the remaining pancakes, cucumber and salmon. Garnish with dill sprigs.

WALNUT & STILTON PANCAKES

Look out for fresh walnuts in the autumn (fall). They are sweet, moist and have none of the dryness that shelled walnuts do. However, you will need a good pair of nutcrackers!

SERVES 4

60 g/2 oz/½ cup plain (all-purpose) flour

60 g/2 oz/½ cup wholemeal (whole wheat) flour

3 tbsp ground walnuts, toasted lightly

1 egg, beaten

1 egg yolk

300 ml/½ pint/1¼ cups milk

1 tbsp oil

salt

1 tbsp walnut oil for brushing

FILLING

175 g/6 oz Stilton (blue) cheese, chopped roughly

1 celery stick, chopped and blanched

3 tbsp chopped walnuts

1 Combine the flours, ground walnuts, and a pinch of salt in a bowl. Make a well in the centre and add the egg, egg yolk, milk and oil. Whisk well and set aside for 30 minutes.

2 Brush a frying pan (skillet) or pancake pan with some of the walnut oil and place over a medium high heat. Tilt the pan and pour in about 50 ml/2fl oz/¼ cup of the batter, tilting the pan immediately in the opposite direction so that the batter coats the base before it sets. Cook for 1 minute until the batter has dried out on top. Turn the pancake over and sprinkle with a little of the Stilton (blue) cheese and celery. Let the cheese melt while the second side cooks for 1 minute.

3 Repeat with the remaining batter, cheese and celery. Makes 8 pancakes.

4 Sprinkle some chopped walnuts over each pancake and roll up. Serve piping hot.

PANCAKES WITH CRABMEAT FILLING

Very good quality crabmeat is available frozen out of the shell, which saves all the bother of preparing the whole crab. It is sold in mixed packs, half brown, half white meat, and is not expensive.

SERVES 4–6

60 g/2 oz/½ cup plain (all-purpose) flour

60 g/2 oz/½ cup wholemeal (whole wheat) flour

1 tsp baking powder

2 eggs, beaten

200 ml/7 fl oz/scant 1 cup milk

2 tbsp oil

FILLING

4 tbsp fresh white breadcrumbs

125 g/4 oz white crabmeat

125 g/4 oz brown crabmeat

2 hard-boiled (hard-cooked) eggs, chopped

2 tbsp mayonnaise

salt and pepper

2 tbsp chopped fresh parsley

1 tsp mustard powder

½ tsp chilli powder

1 Sift the flours and baking powder into a bowl. Make a well in the centre and add the eggs, milk, 1 tablespoon of the oil and seasoning. Whisk together well and leave to rest for 10 minutes.

2 Mix together the breadcrumbs, both crabmeats, the eggs and mayonnaise. Season well.

3 Combine the parsley, mustard powder and chilli powder in a small bowl. Set aside.

4 Brush a frying pan (skillet) or pancake pan with a little of the remaining oil and place over a medium heat. Spoon in 2–3 tablespoons of the batter at a time, to make 7 cm/3 inch diameter pancakes. When the batter has dried out on top, after about 1 minute, turn over and cook for 1 minute. Keep warm in the oven while you make the remaining 11 pancakes.

5 Put 2 or 3 pancakes on each warm serving plate, depending on how hungry

everyone is, and spoon on the
dressed crabmeat. Sprinkle over
a little of the parsley mixture
and serve with a green salad.

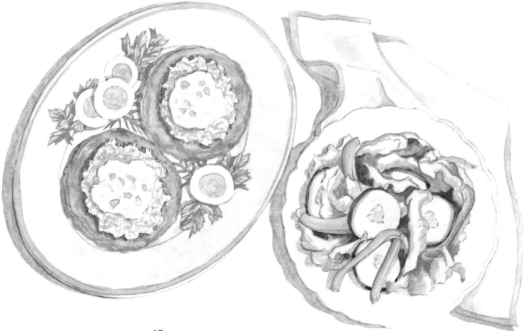

SPRING ASPARAGUS PANCAKES

It is possible nowadays to eat strawberries and asparagus in midwinter and chestnuts in midsummer. But do they taste good? Produce is both cheaper and more tasty in its original season, and summer is the season when the famous English asparagus comes into its own.

SERVES 4

1 quantity Traditional Shrove Tuesday Pancake Batter (see page 4)

24 asparagus stalks, peeled

HOLLANDAISE SAUCE

2 egg yolks

1 tsp malt vinegar

1 bay leaf

250 g/8 oz/1 cup butter, melted and cooled

salt and pepper

1 Add a pinch of salt to the batter and use to make 8 small thick pancakes, about 12 cm/5 inches in diameter. Cover and keep warm.

2 Put the asparagus into a large saucepan of boiling salted water. Blanch for 2–3 minutes, then drain thoroughly. Keep warm.

3 Wrap each pancake around 3 asparagus stalks and set aside on warm plates while you make the Hollandaise sauce.

4 Set a heatproof bowl over a pan of barely simmering water. Put the egg yolks and vinegar into the bowl and whisk until pale. Add the bay leaf. Add the melted butter gradually, whisking all the time until the sauce is thick. Season with pepper. Remove the bay leaf.

5 Put 2 asparagus pancakes on each of 4 warmed serving plates. Spoon over the Hollandaise, and serve warm.

RICOTTA & SPINACH CRESPOLINI

Pancakes are made in different forms around the world and from different flours; this is what the Italians do to them.

1 Grease a round or square casserole, large enough to hold a pancake flat. Add a pinch of salt to the batter and make 6 pancakes (see page 4). Set aside.

2 If using fresh spinach, first put the spinach into a dry saucepan and set over a medium heat. Stir constantly for 2 minutes. Remove from the heat.

3 Combine the spinach, Ricotta (or farmers') cheese, nutmeg, 2 tablespoons of the Parmesan cheese, parsley and tomatoes in a large bowl. Season well. Stir in the flour and eggs.

4 Lay a pancake in the bottom of the casserole and spoon over a fifth of the spinach filling. Layer pancakes and filling alternately, ending with a pancake. Spoon over any leftover filling and sprinkle over the remaining Parmesan cheese. Cover with a lid or foil.

5 Place in a preheated oven at 180°C/350°F/Gas mark 4 for 40 minutes.

6 Cut into 6 wedges and serve immediately, piping hot.

PANCAKES STUFFED WITH CHICKEN & TARRAGON BUTTER

SERVES 4

1 quantity Traditional Shrove Tuesday Pancake Batter (see page 4)

60 g/2 oz/¼ cup butter

350 g/12 oz chicken breasts, cut into strips 5 x 1 x 1 cm/2 x ½ x ½ inches

2 leeks, sliced

4 tbsp chopped fresh tarragon

lamb's lettuce (corn salad) to serve (optional)

salt and pepper

tarragon, to garnish

lemon slices, to garnish

This is a very simple, classic recipe where the taste of the tarragon is really pronounced.

1 Add a pinch of salt to the batter and use to make 8 pancakes (see page 4). Set aside to keep warm.

2 Melt the butter in a frying pan (skillet) and add the chicken and leek. Cook over a medium heat for 5 minutes, stirring frequently. Add the tarragon and season well.

3 Lay 1 pancake flat. Spoon the chicken mixture down the centre of the pancake and it roll up. Repeat with the remaining pancakes.

4 Put the rolled up pancakes on to warmed serving plates and spoon over a little tarragon butter from the pan. Serve with lamb's lettuce (corn salad), or garnish with tarragon and lemon slices, if you prefer.

STIR-FRIED BEEF IN CORIANDER (CILANTRO) ROLL

These quickly cooked pancakes with stir-fried beef can be rustled up in a hurry. Make sure the pancakes are nicely thin and crisp and not at all soggy.

1 Stir the coriander (cilantro) and a pinch of salt into the pancake batter.

2 Brush a frying pan (skillet) or pancake pan with a little of the sunflower oil and place over a medium heat. Tilt the pan and pour in 2 tablespoons of the batter, immediately tilting the pan so that the batter coats the base before it sets. Cook for about 2 minutes on each side. Repeat with the remaining batter, stirring it before making each pancake. Make 8 pancakes. Keep the pancakes warm in a low oven while you make the filling.

3 Heat the sesame oil and remaining sunflower oil in a wok or large frying pan (skillet). Add the spring onions (scallions), (bell) pepper and beef. Stir-fry for 2 minutes and then add the ginger and garlic.

4 Stir in the black bean sauce and cook for 1 minute more. Remove from the heat.

5 Lay a pancake flat. Spoon some filling on to one half of the pancake and fold over other half. Repeat with the remaining pancakes. Put 2 pancakes on each warmed serving plate, garnish with coriander (cilantro) sprigs and serve piping hot.

TRADITIONAL WAFFLES

Waffles are eaten all over the United States, usually served like this. I was converted while staying there, and every morning my landlady would make fresh waffles in front of me for breakfast.

1 Sift the flour and sugar into a bowl. Add the egg yolks, milk, melted butter and vanilla. Whisk together well. Beat the egg whites until stiff. Fold into the waffle batter until thoroughly combined.

2 Heat a waffle iron to medium high and brush with a little melted butter. Pour on

sufficient batter to cover two-thirds of the waffle iron. Close the 2 halves and cook for about 2 minutes, turning over halfway to cook for 1 minute on each side if the waffle iron is a manual one.

3 Turn out on to a warm serving plate. Pour over a little maple syrup and spoon on some vanilla ice cream.

4 The waffles can be made up to 24 hours in advance and reheated in a toaster or under a grill (broiler) before serving.

POTATO WAFFLES WITH GOAT'S CHEESE

SERVES 4

2 eggs, beaten lightly

3 tbsp plain (all-purpose) flour

2 tbsp olive oil

1 large onion, grated

2 large potatoes, grated

60 g/2 oz/1 cup rocket (arugula) leaves

2 tbsp extra virgin olive oil

1 tsp green peppercorns in brine

175 g/6 oz firm goat's cheese, crumbled, or mature (sharp) Cheddar, shaved

3 rashers (slices) streaky bacon, cooked until crisp, chopped finely (optional)

salt and pepper

Waffles are different from pancakes in that they are slightly risen, and they are usually made from a richer batter. They can also be very decorative, especially if you use a waffle iron, which have either a rectangular or a square latticed design, or an attractive heart-shaped design.

1 Whisk together the eggs, flour and 1 tablespoon of the olive oil. Add the grated onion and potatoes.

2 Heat your waffle iron to medium heat and brush with some of the remaining olive oil. Pour in enough batter to cover two-thirds of the hot waffle iron, close the 2 halves together and cook for about 7 minutes, until brown, turning over half way if the waffle iron is a manual one to cook for 3½ minutes on each side. Put on a wire rack to keep warm in a low oven while you make the remaining waffles.

3 Toss the rocket (arugula) leaves in the extra virgin olive oil, seasoning and green peppercorns. Divide between the waffles.

4 Divide the goat's cheese, and bacon if using, between the waffles and serve.

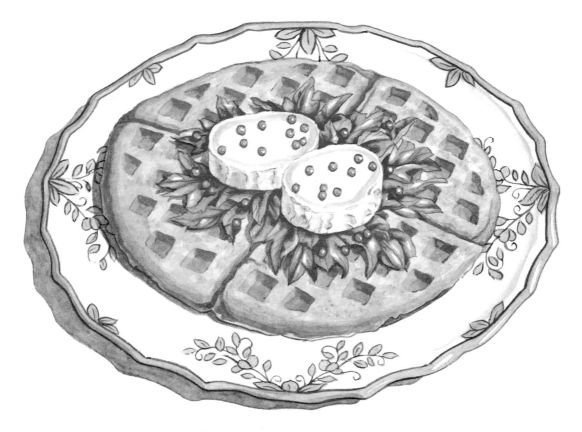

POTATO WAFFLES WITH SMOKED TROUT

SERVES 4

2 eggs, beaten lightly

3 tbsp plain (all-purpose) flour

2 tbsp olive oil

1 large onion, grated

2 large potatoes, grated

5 tbsp mayonnaise

2 tbsp water

1 tbsp wholegrain mustard

250 g/8 oz smoked trout fillets, flaked

4 spring onions (scallions), sliced finely

½ cucumber, peeled and diced

8 gherkins (sweet dill pickles), sliced

salt and pepper

green salad, to serve

After the potatoes have been grated use them instantly or they will go black. For a crisper finish, waffles can be finished in the oven on a wire rack.

1 Whisk together the eggs, flour and 1 tablespoon of the olive oil. Add the onion and potato.

2 Heat your waffle iron to medium heat and brush with the remaining olive oil. Pour in the batter to cover two-thirds of the area. Close the 2 halves and cook for about 7 minutes, turning over half way to cook for 3½ minutes on each side if the waffle iron is a manual one.

3 Transfer to a preheated oven at 160°C/325°F/Gas mark 3 on a wire rack while you make the remaining waffles.

4 Meanwhile, mix the mayonnaise, water and mustard together in a bowl. Add the flaked trout and combine.

5 Put the waffles on to warmed serving plates and divide the trout mayonnaise between them. Sprinkle over the spring onion (scallion), cucumber and gherkins (sweet dill pickles). Season well and serve with a green salad.

CHIVE WAFFLES WITH CREAM CHEESE

Potato waffles are a good base for lots of different herbs and spices – try a pinch of paprika in the mixture, or chopped parsley.

SERVES 4-6

2 eggs, beaten lightly

3 tbsp plain (all-purpose) flour

2 tbsp olive oil

4 tbsp chopped fresh chives

1 large onion, grated

500 g/1 lb white potatoes

salt and pepper

TOPPING

30 g/1 oz/2 tbsp butter

2 leeks, sliced

125 g/4 oz/½ cup full-fat cream cheese

1 egg, beaten

1 tbsp chopped fresh thyme

1 tbsp chopped fresh oregano

salt and pepper

1 Combine the eggs, flour, 1 tablespoon of the olive oil, pepper and chives in a bowl. Stir in the onion and grate the potatoes straight into the bowl.

2 Brush the waffle iron with the remaining olive oil. Heat it to a medium heat and spoon in 4 tablespoons of the waffle batter. Close the 2 halves and cook for about 7 minutes, turning over half way to cook for 3½ minutes on each side if the waffle iron is a manual one.

Transfer to a wire rack and keep warm in the oven while you make the remaining waffles.

3 Melt the butter in a frying pan (skillet) and soften the leeks, about 5 minutes.

4 Mix the cream cheese, egg, thyme, oregano and seasoning together.

5 Put the waffles on to a grill (broiler) rack, spoon on the leeks and the cream cheese mixture, dividing them equally between the waffles, and cook under a preheated grill (broiler) for 4–5 minutes. Serve piping hot.

HORSERADISH BLINIS WITH DILL CREAM

MAKES 80

10 g/¼ oz/2 tsp dried yeast

200 ml/⅓ pint/1 cup warm milk

125 g/4 oz/1 cup wholemeal (whole wheat) flour

salt and pepper

125 g/4 oz/1 cup plain (all-purpose) flour

2 eggs, beaten

3 tbsp melted butter

50 ml/2 fl oz/¼ cup water

1 egg white

oil for brushing

fresh dill sprigs to garnish

DILL CREAM

1 tbsp horseradish relish

500 ml/16 fl oz/2 cups soured cream

1 tsp grated lemon rind

125 g/4 oz/2 cups chopped dill

There are many pancake recipes from around the world, but blinis are unique among them as they are leavened with yeast to give a rich, moist batter. Originating in Russia, they make excellent finger food for parties.

1 Sprinkle the yeast on to the warm milk and set aside for about 15 minutes.

2 Sift the wholemeal (whole wheat) flour and a pinch of salt into a large bowl, make a well in the centre and whisk in the yeast mixture. Cover with clingfilm (plastic wrap) and leave in a warm place until doubled in size, about 20–30 minutes.

3 Sift the plain (all-purpose) flour into a bowl. Make a well in the centre and add the eggs, melted butter and water.

Draw in the flour and beat until smooth. Sir into the wholemeal (whole wheat) flour mixture.

4 Cover the bowl with clingfilm (plastic wrap), and leave it to prove (rise) in the refrigerator overnight.

5 Combine the horseradish relish, soured cream, lemon rind and dill together in a bowl. Season, then cover and chill.

6 Whisk the egg white until stiff and fold into the blini batter until well combined.

34

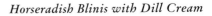

7 Heat a little oil in a frying pan (skillet) or pancake pan. Drop in teaspoonfuls of the batter, 4 at a time, evenly spaced around the pan. Cook over a medium heat for 1–2 minutes and when bubbles rise to the surface, turn over with a palette knife (spatula) and cook for no more than 1 minute. Transfer to a baking sheet, cover and keep warm in a low oven.

8 When the batter is all used, arrange the blinis on a warm serving dish and put small amounts of the dill cream on each one, about ½ teaspoon per blini. Garnish and serve.

LOBSTER BLINIS

SERVES 4

1 quantity Blini mix (see page 34)

1 egg white

TOPPING

15 g/½ oz/1 tbsp butter

1 tbsp plain (all-purpose) flour

2 tbsp single (light) cream

100 ml/3½ fl oz/½ cup milk

¼ tsp chilli powder

1 tbsp brandy

90 g/3 oz/⅓ cup white crabmeat

125 g/4 oz/½ cup lobster meat (if not available use crabmeat)

pepper

TO SERVE

½ iceberg lettuce, shredded

½ cucumber, sliced thinly

2 tomatoes, sliced thinly

4 tbsp chopped fresh parsley

5 lemon slices, halved, to garnish

Blinis are usually served as a sophisticated accompaniment to luxury foods, such as caviar and other roes. Here I have paired larger blinis with a lobster mixture for a delicate lunch dish. Crabmeat can be bought in cans or frozen.

1 Make the blini mix as on page 34, cover and leave overnight in the refrigerator.

2 Next day, melt the butter in a saucepan. Remove from the heat and stir in the flour. Whisk in the cream and milk. Return to the heat and bring to the boil, stirring constantly.

3 Stir in the chilli powder and brandy. Add the crabmeat and lobster meat. Remove from the heat. Sprinkle with pepper, cover and keep warm.

4 Whisk the egg white until stiff and fold into the blini batter until thoroughly combined.

5 Heat a little oil in a frying pan (skillet) or pancake pan. Drop in 2 tablespoons of the batter at a time to make 10 cm/4 inch diameter blinis. When bubbles rise to the surface, after 2–3 minutes, turn over with a palette knife (spatula) and cook for about 1–2 minutes. Keep warm on a baking sheet while you make the remaining blinis.

6 Put 2 blinis, overlapping each other, on each warmed

serving plate. Arrange a quarter of the lettuce, cucumber and tomato together on the side of each plate. Spoon over a quarter of the lobster topping. Sprinkle over some chopped parsley and garnish with a lemon slice. Serve while still warm.

MAKES 80

10 g/¼ oz/2 tsp dried yeast

150 ml/¼ pint/⅔ cup warm milk

125 g/4 oz/1 cup wholemeal (whole wheat) flour

125 g/4 oz/1 cup plain (all-purpose) flour

2 eggs, beaten

3 tbsp melted butter

50 ml/2 fl oz/¼ cup warm milk

50 ml/2 fl oz/¼ cup water

1 egg white

oil for brushing

300 ml/½ pint/1¼ cups soured cream

50 g/2 oz salmon roe

25 g/1 oz lumpfish caviar

salt and pepper

3 lemons, sliced thinly and quartered, to garnish

SALMON ROE CANAPES

This is the classic way to serve blinis. Salmon roe, which is pink, and lumpfish caviar, which is black, are sold in tiny jars in most supermarkets. The caviars look stunning together perched on the soured cream.

1 Make the blini batter as on page 34 and leave overnight in the refrigerator.

2 Next day, beat the egg white until stiff and fold into the mix until thoroughly combined.

3 Brush a frying pan (skillet) or pancake pan with a little oil and heat through. Over a medium-high heat drop in teaspoonfuls of the batter, evenly spaced in the pan. When bubbles rise to the surface, after 1–2 minutes, turn the blinis over with a palette knife (spatula) and cook briefly on the second side.

Keep warm on a covered baking sheet while you make the rest.

4 When all the batter has been used, arrange the warmish blinis on a serving dish and put on to each one about ½ teaspoon of soured cream and a little salmon roe and lumpfish caviar – I find it easiest to pop this on from the end of a teaspoon.

5 Garnish each canapé with a lemon quarter and a sprinkling of pepper.

39

CORNMEAL PONES WITH DOWNHOME BEANS

SERVES 4–6

2 tbsp vegetable oil

1 red onion, chopped

1 green (bell) pepper, chopped

4 rashers (slices) streaky bacon

2 tsp ground coriander

200 g/7 oz chopped tomatoes

1 tbsp tomato purée (paste)

½ tsp chilli flakes

425 g/14 oz cannellini beans

425 g/14 oz borlotti beans

PONES

350 ml/12 fl oz/1½ cups water

175 g/6 oz/1½ cups cornmeal

2 eggs, beaten

250 ml/8 fl oz/1 cup milk

60 g/2 oz/½ cup plain (all-purpose) flour

45 g/1½ oz/3 tbsp butter, melted

salt and pepper

This recipe combines an unleavened cornmeal bread with a delicious bean dish, to make a simple, filling and tasty version of a staple cowboy meal. Use a quick-cook kind of cornmeal.

1 Heat 1 tablespoon of the oil in a large pan and add the onion and green (bell) pepper. Cook for 2 minutes. Chop each bacon rasher (slice) into 4 pieces and add to the pan. Stir in the coriander, chopped tomatoes and tomato purée (paste). Bring to a gentle boil and simmer for 10 minutes.

2 Stir in the chilli flakes. Drain the beans and stir in to the mix. Taste for seasoning. Cover and keep warm over a low heat.

3 Boil the water and put into a bowl. Stir in the cornmeal and salt to taste. Leave to stand for 10 minutes, then add the eggs, beating well. Beat in the milk, flour and butter.

4 Brush a frying pan (skillet) or pancake pan with some of the remaining oil and drop in about 50 ml/2 fl oz/¼ cup of the cornmeal batter. Make sure it does not spread too far. Cook for 2–3 minutes on each side. Keep warm while you make the remaining pones.

5 Put 3 pones on each warmed serving plate and spoon over the beans. Serve piping hot.

NEW ENGLAND FLAPJACK BREAKFAST

SERVES 4

125 g/4 oz/1 cup plain (all-purpose) flour

1 tsp baking powder

1 egg, beaten

1 egg yolk

200 ml/7 fl oz/scant 1 cup milk

2 tbsp melted butter

pinch of salt

FILLING

12 rashers (slices) maple smoked streaky bacon

8 chipolata sausages (optional)

8 eggs

30 g/1 oz/2 tbsp butter

120 ml/4 fl oz/½ cup maple syrup

salt and pepper

Maple syrup – from the sap of the maple tree – and honey are the most natural sweeteners that you can buy. It takes 8 buckets of sap to make 1 bucket of syrup, which explains its high price. Though sweet it is often served with savoury food, especially at breakfast.

1 Sift the flour and baking powder into a bowl. Make a well in the centre and add the egg, egg yolk, milk, 1 tablespoon of the melted butter and a pinch of salt. Whisk together well.

2 Put the bacon and sausages, if using, on a wire rack set over a baking sheet. Place in a preheated oven at 180°C/350°F/Gas mark 4 for 10–12 minutes.

3 Meanwhile, put the eggs and seasoning into a bowl and beat well. Put the butter into a large saucepan.

4 Brush a frying pan (skillet) with the remaining melted butter and spoon in 2 tablespoons of the batter. Do not let it spread to more than 10 cm/4 inches. Cook 3 pancakes at a time, until the batter is used. Stack on a baking sheet and cover to keep warm.

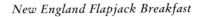

5 To make the scrambled eggs, put the large pan over a gentle heat to melt the butter. Add the eggs and stir constantly for 2 minutes; they will continue cooking while you serve them.

6 Serve 2 chipolatas, if using, 3 rashers (slices) of bacon and a spoonful of scrambled eggs on each plate. Stack 3 pancakes up and transfer to the plate. Serve the maple syrup separately in a jug.

CREPES AU CHOCOLAT

If there are chocoholics among you, you may want to add more melted chocolate to this recipe – but this is enough for me!

1 quantity Traditional Shrove Tuesday Pancake Batter (see page 4)

100 g/3½ oz/3½ squares dark chocolate, melted

1 tbsp caster (superfine) sugar

2 tbsp melted butter

500 g/1 lb/3 cups fresh or frozen raspberries

CUSTARD

600 ml/1 pint/2½ cups milk

90 g/3 oz/⅓ cup caster (superfine) sugar

1 tbsp plain (all-purpose) flour

6 egg yolks

1 Combine the pancake batter with the melted chocolate and 1 tablespoon caster (superfine) sugar.

2 Brush a frying pan (skillet) or pancake pan with a little of the melted butter. Holding the pan over a medium heat, tilt it to one side. Add about 50 ml/ 2 fl oz/¼ cup of the chocolate pancake batter and immediately tilt the pan in the other direction, so that the batter coats the base. Turn the pancake after about 1 minute, to cook the other side briefly, less than a minute. Do not let it burn or cook over too high a heat. Stack on a covered baking sheet to keep warm. Make 8 pancakes.

3 Bring the milk to boiling point, until the surface shivers. Remove from the heat.

4 Whisk together the sugar, flour and egg yolks in a bowl until pale. Add the scalded milk slowly, whisking all the time.

5 Transfer to a pan over a low heat, stir constantly until the mixture thickens. Do not boil. Strain.

6 To serve, spoon custard on to a plate, fold 2 pancakes into quarters and tuck some raspberries into each one. Serve warm.

CREPES SUZETTE

The classic French dessert! If you do flambé the crêpes, spread the flaming liqueur over the whole plate and blow out the flames before the plate gets too hot – but also before all of the alcohol burns off!

SERVES 4–6

1 quantity Traditional Shrove Tuesday Pancake Batter (see page 4)

grated rind of 1 orange

250 g/8 oz/1 cup granulated sugar

150 ml/¼ pint/⅔ cup water

rind of 1 orange, white pith shaved off, cut into thin strips

2 tbsp melted butter

juice of 1 orange

250 ml/8 fl oz/1 cup orange-flavoured liqueur

1 Combine the pancake batter with the grated orange rind. Set aside.

2 Put the sugar and water into a medium saucepan and bring to a gentle boil. Add the strips of orange rind and cook gently until the syrup coats the back of a spoon, about 5 minutes. Set aside.

3 Meanwhile, brush a frying pan (skillet) or pancake pan with a little of the melted butter and place over a medium heat. Tilt the pan and pour in about

50 ml/2 fl oz/¼ cup of the batter, tilting the pan immediately in the opposite direction, so that the batter coats the base. After about 1 minute, or when the batter has dried on top, turn the pancake over and cook on the other side for another minute. Make 8–12 pancakes.

4 Put 2 pancakes flat on each warmed large serving plate.

5 Reheat the syrup and stir in the orange juice and 150 ml/ ¼ pint/⅔ cup of the liqueur.

Pour a little over each plate.

6 Heat the remaining liqueur gently in a small lipped pan. It may ignite itself, but if not, set a match to it and pour over the pancakes immediately. This is most effective if done at the serving table! You can warm the liqueur gently in the kitchen, take it to the table and ignite it. Blow the flames out immediately.

SUMMER FRUIT LAYER

This is based on a traditional Finnish recipe, their version of the British Summer Pudding. The berries can be enjoyed cooked whole with no elaboration, apart from my addition of cream. Put the layers together at the last minute and the flavours will stay distinct.

SERVES 6-8

1 quantity Traditional Shrove Tuesday Pancake Batter (see page 4)

300 g/10 oz/2 cups strawberries, fresh or frozen, halved

300 g/10 oz/2 cups raspberries, fresh or frozen

300 g/10 oz/2½ cups blueberries, fresh or frozen

300 g/10 oz/1½ cups blackcurrants, fresh or frozen

rind of ½ lemon in 1 large piece

4 tbsp icing (confectioners') sugar

125 g/4 oz/½ cup clotted or whipped cream

1 Make 5 pancakes from the pancake batter, as described on page 4.

2 Put half of the fruit into a saucepan with the lemon rind and icing (confectioners') sugar, bring to the boil and simmer for 15–20 minutes, until thick and syrupy. Reserve some uncooked fruit for garnish.

3 Choose a dish with a bit of a lip around the edge to hold the juice from the fruit and put the first pancake on the bottom.

Spoon over the remaining blueberries and 5 tablespoons of the stewed fruit, followed by the second pancake. Spoon over the remaining blackcurrants and 4 tablespoons of the stewed fruit. Put the third pancake on top, spoon over the remaining raspberries and 4 tablespoons of the stewed fruit. Cover with another pancake and the remaining strawberries.

Spoon over 4 tablespoons of the stewed fruit and lay the last pancake on top. Pour over any remaining stewed fruit, and garnish with the reserved uncooked fruit.

4 Cut into wedges, and serve immediately with a little clotted or whipped cream.

ORANGE SOUFFLE PANCAKES

Traditional pancakes are filled with a light, delicately flavoured orange filling for an elegant dessert.

SERVES 4

1 quantity Traditional Shrove Tuesday Pancake Batter (see page 4)

grated rind of 2 oranges

6 tbsp ground hazelnuts, toasted

250 ml/8 fl oz/1 cup milk

2 egg yolks

60 g/2 oz/¼ cup caster (superfine) sugar

3 tbsp plain (all-purpose) flour

4 egg whites

1 Combine the pancake batter with the grated rind of 1 orange. Make 8 large pancakes from the batter, using 2 tablespoonsful for each one, cooking for 1 minute on each side. The pancakes should be fairly thin and delicate.

2 When each pancake has finished cooking, before turning it out of the pan, sprinkle 1 tablespoon of the hazelnuts over it, fold in half and then in half again. Transfer to a baking sheet.

3 Bring the milk nearly to the boiling point, until the surface shivers. Beat together the egg yolks, half of the sugar, the remaining grated orange rind and the flour, until thick. Whisk in the hot milk and return to the milk pan. Bring to the boil and simmer for 2 minutes, whisking constantly. Remove from the heat.

4 Whisk the egg whites until stiff, add the remaining sugar and continue whisking until stiff. Spoon a

quarter of the egg white into the mixture in the pan. Stir well to combine. Add the remaining egg white and fold in lightly until thoroughly combined.

5 Spoon 4 tablespoons of the mixture

underneath the top layer only of each pancake. Place in a preheated oven at 200°C/400°F/ Gas mark 6 for 15 minutes. Serve immediately.

APRICOT PANCAKES

SERVES 4–6

60 g/2 oz/½ cup plain (all-purpose) flour

60 g/2 oz/½ cup wholemeal (whole wheat) flour

1 egg, beaten

1 egg yolk

300 ml/½ pint/1¼ cups milk

1 tbsp oil

500 g/1 lb fresh apricots, halved, stones (pits) removed

90 g/3 oz/⅓ cup caster (superfine) sugar

2 tbsp water

1 tsp ground cinnamon

pinch of ground mace

1 tbsp natural yogurt

oil for brushing

There are times when most of us have to pull our belts in and watch what we eat. This recipe is for those times – healthy but deliciously satisfying.

1 Sift the flours into a bowl. Make a well in the centre and add the egg, egg yolk, milk and oil. Whisk well to combine. Leave to rest for 20–30 minutes.

2 Meanwhile, put the apricots, sugar, water, cinnamon and mace into a saucepan and bring to a gentle boil. Simmer for 10 minutes. Remove half of the apricot halves and set aside. Cook the remaining apricots for a further 10 minutes. Sieve (strain) into a jug and stir in the yogurt. Keep the apricots warm while you make the pancakes.

3 Brush a frying pan (skillet) or pancake pan with a little oil and place over a medium heat. Tilt the pan and pour in about 75 ml/ 3 fl oz/⅓ cup of the batter, tilting the pan immediately in the opposite direction so that the batter coats the base. When the batter has dried on top, after 3–4 minutes, turn the pancake over and cook the other side for about 1 minute. Repeat with the remaining batter to make 6 pancakes.

4 When the pancakes are cooked, slide on to warmed serving plates and spoon a few

whole apricots down the middle
of each one. Roll up the
pancakes and pour over a little
of the apricot sauce.

FLAMBEED BANANA WAFFLES

This is a stunner! Serve it after a barbecue or to end a weekend lunch. The combination of bananas, rum and amaretto biscuits is wonderful.

1 Make 12 waffles (see page 26). Keep warm.

2 Melt the butter in a large frying pan (skillet) and put in the bananas. Increase the heat and cook them for 1 minute, then turn and cook for 1 minute on the other side.

3 Put 2 waffles on each warmed serving plate and lay 1 banana half across each waffle.

4 Add the sugar and water to the pan juices and bring to the boil. Simmer for about 5 minutes until syrupy. Divide the sauce among the 6 plates.

5 Put the rum into a small lipped pan and heat gently. It may ignite by itself, but if it does not, light it with a match and pour a little immediately over each plate. You may be happier to do this in smaller amounts. Blow out the flames

before all the alcohol burns off.
Sprinkle over the amaretto
biscuits if liked, and serve with
ice cream.

CARAMELIZED VANILLA WAFFLES

SERVES 6

½ quantity Traditional Waffle Batter (see page 26)

500 ml/16 fl oz/2 cups vanilla ice cream

250 g/8 oz/1 cup granulated sugar

120 ml/4 fl oz/½ cup water

This is a thrill to make because it produces a wonderful effect, yet is very simple. Handle the hot sugar with care, because it reaches an extremely high temperature.

1 Make 6 waffles following the recipe. Place 1 on each serving plate.

2 Scoop ice cream on to each waffle and put into the freezer or refrigerator while making the sauce.

3 Put the sugar and water into a saucepan and heat gently, stirring, until the sugar has dissolved. Bring to the boil and boil for about 10 minutes, until the sugar turns dark golden brown. Make sure that you do not get any foreign bodies into the sugar as this will make it crystallize, in which case you will have to start again. As an extra precaution, I always brush the side of the pan down with water; this removes any sugar that may stick to it and crystallize, causing the rest of the sugar to do the same.

4 When all of the sugar is this rich dark golden brown colour, remove the waffles from the freezer or refrigerator and pour a little of the caramelized sugar over each one. It will harden instantly on the ice cream and waffle. Serve immediately.

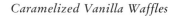

HAZELNUT PRALINE WAFFLES

SERVES 6
1 quantity Traditional Waffle Batter (see page 26)
6 tbsp ground hazelnuts, toasted
30 g/1 oz/2 tbsp butter, melted
500 g/1 lb/2 cups granulated sugar
180 ml/6 fl oz/³⁄₄ cup water
4 tbsp chopped hazelnuts
120 ml/4 fl oz/¹⁄₂ cup single (light) cream
500 ml/16 fl oz/2 cups vanilla ice cream

Do not be put off by the amount of sugar in this recipe; it is the smallest amount to use that is practical to make a praline and a caramel sauce.

1 Combine the waffle batter and ground hazelnuts. Heat your waffle iron to medium high and brush with melted butter. Pour on enough batter to cover two-thirds of the iron and close the 2 halves. Cook for 2 minutes, turning over half way to cook for 1 minute on each side if the waffle iron is a manual one. Turn out on to a wire rack, and make 5 more waffles.

2 Put 250 g/8 oz/1 cup of the sugar into a saucepan with 75 ml/3 fl oz/¹⁄₃ cup of the water. Bring to the boil and simmer gently until it starts to change colour to golden brown. In order to catch it at the right stage, when the colour reaches a dark brown, drop a little on to a plate; if it turns rock hard, it is ready. Stir in the chopped hazelnuts and pour on to a metal baking sheet. It should harden quite quickly.

3 Put the remaining sugar and water into a saucepan and bring to the boil. Simmer gently until the sugar changes colour. Have ready a large bowl of iced water. When the syrup reaches a golden colour, about 20 minutes, remove from the heat and put

the base of the pan into the cold water to prevent any further cooking. Stir in the cream and leave to set.

4 When the praline has set, break into small pieces, using a toffee hammer or wooden mallet.

5 Put one waffle on to each plate, top with vanilla ice cream and pour over 4 tablespoons of the sauce. Serve immediately, decorated with the praline.

EXOTIC FRUIT WAFFLES WITH CARDAMOM CREAM

This is for grown-ups only! The sophisticated, fragrant combination of flavours will stun your guests. Passion fruit purée can be substituted for the fresh passion fruit. Any mix of exotic fruits can be used in the topping.

SERVES 6

15 passion fruit

½ quantity Traditional Waffle Batter (see page 26)

30 g/1 oz/2 tbsp butter, melted

125 g/4 oz/½ cup sugar

150 ml/¼ pint/⅔ cup water

1 mango

10 lychees, canned or fresh, peeled and stoned (pitted)

1 starfruit, cut into 12 slices

seeds from 9 crushed cardamom pods

300 ml/½ pint/1¼ cups whipping cream

1 Halve 12 of the passion fruit and press the flesh through a sieve (strainer) into a bowl. Stir the purée into the batter.

2 Heat the waffle iron to medium and brush with some of the melted butter. Pour on enough batter to cover two-thirds of the iron and close the 2 halves. Cook for about 3 minutes, or 1½ minutes on each side if the waffle iron is a manual one. Turn out on to a wire rack and keep warm in a low oven. Repeat to make 6 waffles.

3 Put the sugar and water into a saucepan and bring to a gentle boil, stirring frequently, to make a syrup. Cut the remaining passion fruit in half and press the flesh through a sieve (strainer) into the syrup. Peel the mango and cut the flesh from the stone (pit) in chunks. Add to the syrup. Add the lychees and starfruit, and simmer for 5 minutes.

4 Remove the fruit with a slotted spoon and set aside. Boil the remaining syrup for 5 minutes until it thickens slightly.

5 Put the cardamom seeds into a bowl with the whipping cream. Whip until the cream just holds its own shape.

6 To serve, put a waffle on each serving plate, spoon over some fruit and syrup and spoon on whipped cream.

CHERRIES JUBILEE STACK

The grand finale! This is the greatest waffle of them all, and will bring gasps of delight at the table, where I defy any one person to finish a whole stack. This is a wonderful treat to give to children on the last day of the holidays.

SERVES 4

1 quantity Traditional Waffle Batter (see page 26)

750 g/1½ lb fresh cherries, stoned (pitted) and rinsed, or 2 x 400 g/14 oz cans of pitted cherries in heavy syrup, drained and syrup reserved

125 g/4 oz/½ cup granulated sugar

150 ml/¼ pint/⅔ cup water

500 ml/16 fl oz/2 cups vanilla ice cream

1 Make 12 waffles from the batter. Turn out on to a wire rack and keep warm in a low oven.

2 If using fresh cherries, put the sugar and water into a saucepan and bring to the boil. When the sugar has dissolved, add the cherries and simmer until soft, about 10 minutes. Remove the cherries with a slotted spoon and reserve. Return the syrup to the boil and simmer for 8–10 minutes, until slightly thickened.

3 If using canned cherries, put 150 ml/¼ pint/⅔ cup of the reserved syrup and the sugar into a saucepan, bring to the boil and simmer for 12–15 minutes, then add the cherries.

4 Put a waffle on each serving plate and a scoop of vanilla ice cream, followed by another waffle and scoop of vanilla ice cream and topped by a third waffle and scoop of ice cream. Spoon over a quarter of the

cherries and sauce. Serve
immediately.

INDEX